PAUL ECONOMEN

Let the Cat Out of the Bag

Idioms and Idioms to make you a hit at work, school, weddings and more

First edition

Editing by Jean Marie

This book was professionally typeset on Reedsy.
Find out more at reedsy.com

Contents

1

Introduction

Why should you care about idioms? Because English is woven into most of our global culture. It's a necessary element of most commerce and marketing. It is the third most spoken language on this planet.

Yet, it's also a complex language. Navigating through its subtleties can be a real adventure itself.

So anyone who wants to learn English or use it more effectively had better know about idioms. There are over 25,000 English idioms, so it isn't often that one completes a sentence without using one.

What is an idiom?

Its name derives from the Greek *idioumai,* meaning "particular to oneself." By way of example, take the word "bang." As a noun, it's a loud noise. "Buck" is slang for a one-dollar bill.

But when we combine those two words, as in "more bang for your buck," they take on a third meaning: "a greater return for your money." We show you how it changes.

And then we complete your understanding of this "third word" by providing its origin. This will also help you to avoid embarrassment by using it correctly. When the true origins are illusive, I'll go with the most plausible.

I've also avoided idioms or origins that did not seem suitable for a G-rated audience. And likewise, I've tried to put it all into simple English, so a PhD is not required to benefit from this book.

What's in it for you?

- Expanding your knowledge by growing your vocabulary
- Understanding and appreciating everyday language by getting the subtleties and the diversity of this language.
- Impressing the crowd. Maybe you just want to show off—that certain someone, your boss, your prospect, your teacher or complete strangers.

Look at it this way: grammar and such are the meat. You've got that. Idioms are the steak sauce.

And you will be in better command of the language with this handy pocket guide, be it on the street, at home or anywhere people are talking.

So, a book dealing with each one would have its own zip code. That's why I've chosen those that seemed most appropriate and most useful.

So have fun!

2

Workplace Idioms

The mailroom is only a few floors away from ultimate business power, celebrity status and a staff of 20 to mind every detail of your Beverly Hills 40-room cottage. These idioms may help you arrive:

Game plan

The Board of Directors needed a new strategy to accomplish the upcoming merger. They outlined 10 different actions needed to make sure the merger went smoothly. That was their game plan.

Much like a coach's pre-game football plans to win the big game.

Learn the ropes

A trainee would need to see how things function in his new company position. His own job requirements in the mail room, the office politics and anything else required to make sure he would someday be Chief Executive Officer. He has to learn the ropes.

Sounds like an old sailing ship, doesn't it? Every new recruit had to learn the names of every rope as well as the function of the rigging, forestays and wires and how they related to each other.

Across the board

Business owner J. P Withers wants to give a two percent cost-of-living increase to his good buddies at Withers & Company. Well, of course he can't do that. He would have to give it to each employee—from the President to the janitor. Equally spread across the company organizational board, as it were.

This saying came from horse racing. Hapless Joe would bet $20 on the same horse to win, place or show.

Red tape

You're heading the committee to build a new company plant in Leaky Drain, Wisconsin. Deadline is next week, so you really need to get the ball rolling (remember that earlier idiom?) but you keep running into government bureaucracy.

The Department of Departments requires you to file a Form 3409W(b) in triplicate then submit it at 3:17 pm—blah, blah, blah.

You can mutter to King Charles V, who, some 400 years ago, wanted to prioritize his administrative documents. So, his staff put red ribbons (or tape) around the most urgent ones. Soon that filing system was all the rage in other countries.

Rock the boat

To successfully climb those corporate ladder rungs, one must never say or do anything to upset or cause trouble within the existing structure of that organization.

That's just as insane as fishing on the open sea with a few friends and you suddenly stand up and start to rock your vessel to and fro.

This idiom came from William Jennings Bryan, American politician and statesman, who said in 1914 "The man who rocks the boat ought to be stoned when he gets back on shore."

Take the bull by the horns

One surefire way to impress upper management is to take the initiative. Sometimes you can't wait around while all the chaos and disorder calms down and everything falls into place. Because it usually won't. in fact, it will probably get worse.

You have to act and act now, no matter how dangerous the situation seems.

Wasn't really so different back in the Wild West, when a cowboy had to control a rampaging bull who was knocking down fences and tearing up your fields.

You can't wait until the bull gets tired. You have to grab it by the horns and wrestle it to the ground.

Ahead of the pack

Snivel & Sons stays ahead of the competition by offering neon widgets in three different sizes. Even those foreign pack of wolves are left behind because they cannot compete with that extensive array. Snivel & Sons are always the market leader.

Another possible origin of that idiom says it refers to horse racing or dog racing—where you are always the lead animal.

See eye to eye

You took some time off from your sales job to run for an important city position—dog catcher.

Okay, so maybe it's not a limos-and-mudslinging kind of job. But you love dogs and want to see they get treated lovingly in their new homes.

Your opponent is also a dog lover. Veronica has several pooches at home and treats them all like kings.

So, when it comes to humane and loving treatment of animals, you and Veronica see eye to eye.

That saying evolved from a Biblical passage—Book of Isaiah, which implies a physical face-to-face at exactly the same level.

3

Marketing Idioms

Everything—product or service—has to be sold—but first, it has to be marketed. Whether it is a corny commercial of dancing mice or talking tobacco leaves, promotion needs to make consumers aware of something they cannot live without.

Hopefully, these few idioms will aid in getting those chocolate covered tire covers to their proper owners.

Go the extra mile

Sure, everyone knows you're just a gas station attendant. But what if you not only pumped gas for the customer, but you also washed their windshield and checked their tire pressure.

You just went the extra mile by doing more than was expected of you by the customer and the boss.

But its origin did not have quite the same meaning. Jesus, in the Book of Matthew in the New Testament, said "Whoever forces you to go one mile, go with them two." He meant that one should bear their burden with generosity and cheer.

Touch base

Now that you are well again, your boss wants to go over the new ad campaigns with you so you have the latest sales script and such. As the word "touch" implies, your meeting with her will be brief.

This, like a lot of American sayings, stems from our national pastime of baseball. To qualify as a run and not be tagged by the opposite team, the runner has to touch the base.

Raise the bar

Your widgets are so good, they will raise the standard of excellence for the widget industry. Every widget maker who wants to survive will have to rise to your level of quality.

This concept evolved from certain sports. Specifically, pole vaulting and high jumps. They compete with other highly-skilled athletes for the medals.

To do that, they will always put up the bar a notch after each jump. If they succeed in vaulting over a record height, every other athlete has to do the same to effectively compete.

Back to square one

Well, that last ad campaign with dancing eggs went flat. Now, you have to start all over again.

Yep, another sports reference. This time, it's football. Before TV, radio listeners in the 1930s had to rely on radio commentators for visuals.

So, these announcers mentally divided up the field into numbered grids then used those squares in the grid to describe the plays.

They considered the front of the home team's goal to be Square One. As the players moved up and down the field, they went into different grids. And when the home team kicked the ball toward their goal, they went back to Square One.

At that point, they started all over at the first down.

Ballpark figure

How many buyers will this ad campaign draw? You don't know exactly, but you can estimate it, based on last year's campaign, current buying trends and other factors.

Again with the sports. How many attendees showed up for today's baseball game? Well, we can't count heads, but we can give you an approximate count. Yep, a ballpark figure.

No strings attached

You give an advertiser a small token for getting you some good ad rates. It's not bribery; the gift carries no ulterior motives—hidden or otherwise. The lucky recipient was not obligated in any way. No strings attached.

One source says that phrase came from the cloth industry. Any flaws in the fabric were marked with a string so it would not be overlooked.

Jump through hoops

Remember that time you wanted a new house? Perfect location, right price, plenty of room.

Then the mortgage company demanded all kinds of documents—soil tests, flood plain reports, rodent control proof. Seems like they made you jump through a lot of hoops to get that loan.

If you felt like a circus animal in the ring leaping through the fiery hoops and a cracking whip nearby, you got the idea.

Don't look a gift horse in the mouth

Giving horses as gifts has gone out of style. However, if you ever get one from an eccentric, wealthy client, just say thank you and at least act thrilled.

Here's why. It seems that, as horses age, their teeth grow longer. Chances are, a younger horse is a better deal than an older one.

But it would be the height of ungratefulness if someone handed you the reins to a beautiful stallion, you promptly opened up his mouth and pointed to his long teeth. Don't ever do that, okay?

Now, sell your horse trailer and retire to Miami.

Down the drain

Have you ever accidently pulled the plug in the sink and watched your priceless ring go round and round before disappearing down the drain?

Hopefully not.

But it could happen to you figuratively. Anything of value that has been wasted. A new car that just fell apart. Oh, and those singing bears for that bankrupt ice chest client. Had to send them back to the zoo. All that money you spent went down the drain.

Oh, yeah. This idiom has a close cousin: down the tubes.

Word-of-mouth

In social media terms, it means the best kind of advertising possible. How is that?

Paid promotion, whether in print, online or TV, can be effective, but a customer who, on their own, opens their mouth to give you words of praise about your product—well, that testimonial is much more valuable.

Because this kind of promotion is not some actor reading a script or mouthing a tired cliché. It is heartfelt and honest. Something the public can really relate to. And it is free!

This idiom originated from the Latin phrase *viva voce*, literally "living voice."

The big picture

While the actions of a sales crew may consider only the immediate gain, the decisions of a CEO must consider the overall, long-term effects of their marketplace or how it might influence the global economy. They have to consider the larger scope of a situation or issue.

It comes from an article in *Time Magazine* of 1977, which spoke of extroverts who caused problems in a "haste to paint the big picture."

Land an account

Your marketing agency has been courting Dithers & Company as an account for some time now. You finally landed them. They are now your client.

The word "land" derives from the Old English word *lendan*, "to bring ashore." In the mid 1850s, this word was applied to other areas.

In the long run

Now that you have landed Dithers & Company, you need to create a marketing campaign that will last for a long time to be successful. After all, it may not produce enough income for you or them in just a few months. They must be willing to stick with you for the long run—at least a year.

This one apparently alludes to a runner who needs to run the full five miles in order to have success.

4

Wedding Idioms

T he next time you are asked to toast the wedded couple at the reception, you can confidently sprinkle your good wishes and off-color references with a few idioms about their blissful future. Try these:

Tie the knot

Another way to say "get married." It derives from a wedding tradition that goes way back: the handfasting ceremony. This medieval Celtic practice symbolically binds the couple together by tying knots of cloth around their hands. And so two become one.

Get hitched

This other way to say "get married" emerged in the 1500s in Europe but originally referred to horses being attached to a wagon. By the time it had reached America, this concept also had to do with two people becoming one.

Pop the question

You've finally got up the nerve to get hitched. If you're old fashioned, you get down on one knee and hand her a delicate flower as you ask her to marry you. The questioned is now popped.

This phrase came about in the early 1700s but had other connotations. Its marriage related sense developed about 100 years later.

Take the plunge

You walk up to the edge of the pool. Lots of other people splash, dive and swim in the water. You hesitate—is it too cold? Will I drown? Your friends egg you on with colorful words like "chicken" and "scaredy cat". Finally, you dive in.

Getting married can be like that fearful pool. If you then just propose to your special someone, you've now committed to taking on that daunting task—you've taken the plunge.

5

Animal Idioms

We can't forget our beastly buddies who give us unconditional love. Here are some idioms in their honor.

The elephant in the room

There's George, calmly sitting on his couch, enjoying his umpteenth rerun of *Taxicab Murders*. That famous detective twirls his moustache before he announces the guilty party.

George notices a huge, four-legged pachyderm demolishing his living room. He chooses to ignore it completely.

Something similar happened in the 1800s where a man in a fable called the Inquisitive Man was so entranced by all the magnificent items at a museum that he failed to notice an elephant in the room.

Apparently, it happens a lot. Thus the expression, which says that nobody is willing to talk about a huge problem right before them.

Wet behind the ears

Your new assistant is untrained—in most everything. They don't seem to function well in a business environment. Total lack of judgement.

They're probably a lot like a newborn calf, who has just arrived and is soaking wet. Mom has cleaned him but that little dip behind the ears is still moist.

Get someone's goat

Some people really know how to irritate others. It's almost as if they went to school to learn how.

Here's another saying from horse racing. Goats have been known to calm down thoroughbred horses. To calm down a skittish horse, its owner would put a goat in the horse's stall on the night before the race.

Ah, but some nasty competitors would steal the goat, which would then agitate the horse and hopefully lose the race.

Don't know about you, but that would certainly get my goat.

6

School Idioms

You're headed for the principal's office. Your teacher wasn't amused when you told her your dog devoured your essay on the works of great English authors—for the fifth time.

How about some idioms to toss out during your reprimand as Principal Cheaver gives you that disdaining look?

Draw a blank

You're eagerly reading your homework when you go to get a snack and realize you can't remember what you read. You've just drawn a blank.

You can thank Queen Elizabeth the First, who established a national lottery in 1567. Participants put their names on a slip of paper which were then put into a pot, while an equal number of slips, some blank and others with participants names on them, went into another pot.

Pairs of tickets were drawn at the same time from the pots, which matched a participant to a prize. But, just like your chances in Las Vegas, most drew a blank slip.

Pass with flying colors

On your journey to graduate, you would not just squeak by your studies, you would sail in the classroom with head held high and pass each course with an A+.

Yep, it's a nautical term from the 1700s. A ship's colors are its flags. As it sailed into port victoriously for one reason or another, its flags would be fully unfurled as it passed through.

Eager beaver

In much the same way as above, you would not just do the homework required, you would enthusiastically organize it all and label everything neatly. All this while your teacher gets an earful of rah! Rah!

This saying evolved in the early 1900s when some recruits in the armed forces would do anything to impress their commanding officers. Beavers, of course, are noted for building dams many times their size.

Learn something by heart

If you really want to impress Ms. Mushkins in your theatre class, you need to go beyond cue cards and cheat sheets. You need to study that Shakespeare soliloquy until every word, every nuance, every emotion comes from you without thinking.

You need to own it. Know it by heart.

Okay, so why the heart? Isn't this a brain thing? Because the ancient Greeks considered that organ to be the seat of one's memories, thoughts and emotion.

Bookworm

These days, a lot of people aren't even sure what book is. So, if you even read them, you might be called—and not in a nice way—to someone who passionately devours the printed page.

But they may not realize the word came about because there are real insects, such as silverfish, book lice and beetles who literally live between the pages.

Copycat

Someone who imitates others in deed or thought. They may mimic their actions or downright plagiarize.

But how could a cute, cuddly kitty do that? Because long ago, a "cat" was actually a term of contempt. The term came from one Constance Harrison, whose 1887 memoir referred to a plagiarist as a "copycat."

Can't teach an old dog new tricks

If someone has been using a flip phone for years, it might be impossible for you to try and have them learn the ways of smart devices. They will be cranky, resistive and take forever, if they do get it.

Kind of like an old hound dog who just lays around. Won't sit, roll over or even move. They will probably be completely hopeless.

At least, John Fitzherbert thought so, when he wrote about these creatures in his book "The Boke of Husbandry" in 1534. Which may give it the prize as the world's oldest idiom.

Play hooky

Sure, you're supposed to show up for that test in your Classical Literature class. You can skip class, you can fail to appear as scheduled or you can give it all a bit more whimsy and simply "play hooky."

Its origin is hazy, but one likely root comes from the Dutch slang word *hoekie,* which translates into "hide and seek."

7

Sales Idioms

You've got to admire your sales force. An unwavering army of promoters who will get in front of anyone, anytime to show them the many advantages of blue-handled widgets. They have their own language, too. And here are some suggestions:

Take it to the bank

A mortgage broker hands you a certified check for $4,000. He could have given you cash, because both will be accepted by your bank without question.

Later, salesman Dave on your team brags that he's about to get an order for 10,000 blue widgets. "It's a done deal," he says. "You can take it to the bank."Hmm. That's less certain, knowing Dave.

The expression was popularized in the 1970s TV show *Baretta*. It's cousin, "bank on it" has been around since the early 1900s.

Hit the ground running

With this one, there is no slowing down. Assuming the Sales Manager had done his job correctly, his sales crew wouldn't miss a beat when they hit the ground running.

This one evolved from parachute teams, who had to spring into action quickly when they dropped amongst their enemy forces.

Bend over backwards

You really want to help your client get the full benefit of your widgets, you call them up, you pay them a visit and give a personal demonstration of your product. You would bend over backwards for them.

Sounds just like a gymnastic reference—especially one going way back to 900 A.D.

Hands down

Your widget has the lowest price, superior quality and an unconditional money-back guarantee. You can beat your competition unquestionably. Yes, you can beat them hands down.

Funny, because that's the origin of that saying. When a horse was lengths ahead of the rest, the jockey might loosen his grip on the reins and drop his hands as he gallops across the finish line.

The ball is in your court

Your prospect has laid out their counteroffer. They were quite specific about what color widget they want, when they want to take delivery and what costs they are willing to pay. They now wait for you to make a move; the ball is in your court.

Feel like you're playing a tennis game? You should that's where the phrase came from.

8

Everyday Idioms

We suddenly realized that we had a lot of idioms lying around that didn't seem to fit anywhere else, so we just tossed them in here. But that's good for you because they have a lot of versatility. Parties, birthdays, tailgate meets. Get creative.

Hit the nail on the head

To identify a solution or a problem exactly. Sales had slumped and Agent Suzie Jones looked at the sales graph, looked at previous week's sales and hit the nail on the head when she saw that the agents were spending too much time on paperwork.

Undoubtedly a carpentry reference.

Wet blanket

These days, you can be a buzzkill or simply someone who puts the fire out of someone's enthusiasm or enjoyment.

Which would be appropriate, since cooks kept a damp blanket handy to smother any kitchen fires that tried to have fun.

Get up on the wrong side of the bed

Your Sales Manager has been in a grumpy mood all day. He barked at everyone at the sales meeting. He obviously got up on the wrong side of the bed.

Say what?

He should have listened to the ancient Romans. Philosophers there saw the right side of a bed (and everything else, actually) as a positive thing. But that left side? Oohh! Time for an anti-evil incantation.

Everything but the kitchen sink

Why the kitchen sink was left out is unknown, but this phrase implies that everything else is included. Like our top salesman George, who dragged out every gimmick he had—everything but the kitchen sink.

The saying found its way into the Syracuse Herald in 1918. Then, it became popular during World War II, as an indication of what we might throw at the enemy to make them surrender.

Play by ear

Musicians who had no written sheets of music learned to play by listening to the various sounds. Likewise, a speaker without a pitch or a sample will have to listen to what his crowd says, noting their every emotion and body language.

If he was a real good listener, he could then play it by ear and shift directions as needed.

Start the ball rolling

To put something into action. It supposedly comes from the game of croquet.

In order to get the silent auction going, you could nudge that person next to you out of a nap and have them shout out a number. Or maybe not.

Add fuel to the fire

Okay, your Uncle Julius is already sore with you because you forgot to pick him up at the airport. Then he asked you to buy his dinner and you thought he said "winner." Now he's steaming—you just made a bad situation worse.

It's as if you took a gallon of gasoline and poured it on a roaring flame.

This saying comes from an ancient Roman historian, Titus Livius, whose observations about ambition and youth.

Piece of cake

You just got a score of 100% on difficult test. For you, it was a piece of cake. (that should impress someone, even if that someone is you).

The saying started with the Royal Air Force in the 1930s. that's all the details known for sure. Over and out.

Read between the lines

You meet up with an old friend who's been out of town for a while. Swapping stories of the past and catching up. How's the wife, you ask.

He implies it's all good but best buddies are straightforward with each other. You get the feeling all is not well, He forces a smile. You have to search for a hidden meaning in his words.

All very cryptic. You have to read between the lines of what he is saying and get the real story.

Not unlike a scene where Sherlock reads a supposedly innocent letter from the prime suspect detailing a recent vacation to the vineyards of France.

But the wise Mr. Holmes examines the lines of type closer to find a coded message buried within, meant for his spy ring.

The saying was first found in an 1862 edition of the *New York Times*.

Cool as a cucumber

Those delicious, green vegetables always feel soft and cool, right?

Well, British poet John Gay thought so, and said as much in his poem "New Song of New Similes" In 1732.

That eventually came to describe someone's calm demeanor under stressful circumstances. Like all the seniors just after finals.

In the bag

That's when you are so confident about something, you're almost smug about it. Want to be class president? It's in the bag.

It's a baseball thing. Around the early 1900s, when the New York Giants were so confident of winning a game, they would haul their ball bag off the field early, knowing that they could not possibly lose the game.

Get a kick out of something

What's your favorite ice cream? When you have a coneful of that frozen dessert, you get a kick out of lapping up that double scoop.

And you can thank song writer Cole Porter, who composed "I Get a Kick Out of You" in 1934 for popularizing that saying.

Cross your fingers

Facing a difficult test, you need all the help you can get. You might take your finger and slip it over your other finger for good luck.

You have a lot of history behind you. Before Christianity, one could put their index finger over another's finger to show support to them. This encouraged good spirits and anchored a wish until it came true. That evolved into one crossing their own fingers.

Let the cat out of the bag

Sometimes you just have to tell someone a secret that you swore you would never divulge. But once you've blabbed, there goes the cat.

In the Middle Ages, dishonest livestock sellers would hand their victim a bag supposedly with a live pig inside.

Once the duped buyer got home and opened the bag, he would discover a common cat inside, instead of the more expensive pig he had paid for.

Take with a grain of salt

You should probably keep a pound of salt nearby when you watch the commercials, lest your mind be poisoned. That's because this saying advises you to keep a bit of skepticism with everything you see or hear.

Or eat, in this case. Salt makes everything more palatable. Ancient Roman author Pliny the Elder translated an ancient text which advised that salt be taken with food for a slightly more important reason: it could be an antidote for poison.

Get off one's high horse

Arrogance is a learned skill with some people. They exude a pompous and self-righteous air with every word they say. They must think they are a king.

With good reason, as medieval royalty and soldiers would often ride around on large horses just to let the peasants know who runs the show.

Now you can just tell these snooty types to dismount and join the rest of the crowd.

9

Conclusion

Again, this book is just a taste of the many idioms of the American English language. It is meant to give a few examples of the broad use of this form of communication.

You will be more in command of English and as such, able to use it to your advantage in many areas of life. Your vocabulary will also increase.

But above all that, learning and using idioms puts you more in tune with the culture, since idioms have been created and used exclusively by that culture.

You can liken it to learning Spanish in a middle American high school as opposed to packing up and moving to Costa Rica for five years.

And there is no end to online sources for idioms. They are all free and informative so hit the search bar.

Now, you should give a review of this book. If you found it helpful, please tell is specifically how it helped you.

I welcome all comments. I strive for accuracy, but sometimes I mess up. So, if you've found additional information on an idiom or if you know that an origin listed is inaccurate, please let me know.

If you would like to have a second book of idioms, what subjects should I include?

If you found this book helpful, I would be very appreciative if you left a favorable review for this book on Amazon.

10

References

40 Bizarre Yet Funny English Idioms to Help You Sound Like a Native Speaker. (2021, September 28). My English Routine. Retrieved September 15, 2022, from https://myenglishroutine.com/funny-english-idioms/

50 common business idioms. (2018, June 7). topcorrect.com Blog. Retrieved September 15, 2022, from https://www.topcorrect.com/blog/50-common-business-idioms/

68 Examples of Idioms for Kids. (n.d.). Retrieved September 15, 2022, from https://examples.yourdictionary.com/idioms-for-kids.html

across the board. (n.d.). Retrieved September 15, 2022, from https://www.theidioms.com/across-the-board.

Admin, C. (2019, August 21). *15 Marketing Idioms in English.* CISL English Language Schools, California. Retrieved September 15, 2022, from https://cisl.edu/15-marketing-idioms-in-english/

Bank on it and take it to the bank Idiom Definition. (2022, July 6).

GRAMMARIST. Retrieved September 15, 2022, from https://gram marist.com/idiom/bank-on-it-and-take-it-to-the-bank

big picture. (n.d.). In *TheFreeDictionary.com*. Retrieved September 15, 2022, from https://idioms.thefreedictionary.com.

Chalmers, T. (2018, July 2). *Where Does the Phrase 'Tie the Knot' Come From?* Culture Trip. Retrieved September 15, 2022, from https://thecu lturetrip.com/europe/united-kingdom/scotland/articles/where-does-the-phrase-tie-the-knot-come-from/

Copycat | Phrase Definition, Origin & Examples. (n.d.). Retrieved September 15, 2022, from https://www.gingersoftware.com/conte nt/phrases/copycat/

Definition and etymology of land. (n.d.). Etymonline. Retrieved September 15, 2022, from https://www.etymonline.com/word/land

Definition of down the drain. (n.d.). In *www.dictionary.com*. Retrieved September 15, 2022, from https://www.dictionary.com/browse/down -the-drain

Definition of idiom. (n.d.). In *www.dictionary.com*. Retrieved September 15, 2022, from https://www.dictionary.com/browse/idiom

Definition of in the long run. (n.d.). In *www.dictionary.com*. Retrieved September 15, 2022, from https://www.dictionary.com/browse/in-the -long-run.

   eager beaver. (n.d.). Retrieved September 15, 2022, from https://www .theidioms.com/eager-beaver.

English idioms | EF | United States. (n.d.). Retrieved September 15, 2022, from https://www.ef.edu/english-resources/english-idioms/

Get up on the wrong side of the bed and wake up on the wrong side of the bed Idiom Definition. (2022, August 7). GRAMMARIST. Retrieved September 15, 2022, from https://grammarist.com/idiom/get-up-on-the-wrong-side-of-the-bed-and-wake-up-on-the-wrong-side-of-the-bed.

Go the extra mile Idiom Definition. (2022, August 9). GRAMMARIST. Retrieved September 15, 2022, from https://grammarist.com/idiom/go-the-extra-mile/

Hands Down | Phrase Definition, Origin & Examples. (n.d.). Retrieved September 15, 2022, from https://www.gingersoftware.com/content/phrases/hands-down/

Hello English. (2016, January 29). *Birthday Phrases and Party Idioms.* Retrieved September 15, 2022, from https://helloenglish.com/article/94/Birthday-Phrases-and-Party-Idioms

High horse - Definition, Meaning & Synonyms. (n.d.). In *Vocabulary.com.* Retrieved September 15, 2022, from https://www.vocabulary.com/dictionary/high horse.

Idiom: Ahead of the pack (meaning & examples). (n.d.). Oyster English. Retrieved September 15, 2022, from https://www.oysterenglish.com/idiom-ahead-of-the-pack.html

Idiom of the day: Draw A Blank | Learn English. (n.d.). Retrieved September 15, 2022, from https://www.ecenglish.com/learnenglish/lessons/idiom-day-draw-a-blank.

Ilyas, N. (2018, November 20). *42 English Idioms Related to School and Education* MyEnglishTeacher.eu Blog. Retrieved September 15, 2022, from https://www.myenglishteacher.eu/blog/english-idioms-related-to-school/

In the Bag | Phrase Definition, Origin & Examples. (n.d.). Retrieved September 15, 2022, from https://www.gingersoftware.com/content/phrases/in-the-bag/

Jones, B. (2022, February 11). *30 Marriage and Wedding Idioms.* Get More Vocab. Retrieved September 15, 2022, from https://getmorevocab.com/30-marriage-and-wedding-idioms/

Jones, M. (2022, February 9). *Where Does the Phrase "Let the Cat Out of the Bag" Come From?* Reader's Digest. Retrieved September 15, 2022, from https://www.rd.com/article/let-the-cat-out-of-the-bag.

Jump through hoops Idiom Definition. (2022, July 20). GRAMMARIST. Retrieved September 15, 2022, from https://grammarist.com/idiom/jump-through-hoops
    "Learn it off by heart." - phrase meaning and origin. (n.d.). © Gary Martin. Retrieved September 15, 2022, https://www.phrases.org.uk/bulletin_board/42/messages/687.html

Martin, G. (n.d.). *"Take with a grain of salt" - the meaning and origin of this phrase*. Phrasefinder. Retrieved September 15, 2022, from https://www.phrases.org.uk/meanings/take-with-a-grain-of-salt.

no strings attached. (n.d.). Retrieved September 15, 2022, from https://www.phrases.com/phrase/no-strings-attached_5516

Pass with flying colors Idiom Definition. (2022, July 20). GRAMMARIST. Retrieved September 15, 2022, from https://grammarist.com/idiom/pass-with-flying-colors/

Pearson. (2021a, November 2). *Cool as a Cucumber - Meaning, Usage and Origin.* English-Grammar-Lessons.com. Retrieved September 15, 2022, from https://english-grammar-lessons.com/cool-as-a-cucumber-meaning.

Pearson. (2021b, November 24). *Ballpark Figure - Meaning, Origin and Usage.* English-Grammar-Lessons.com. Retrieved September 15, 2022, from https://english-grammar-lessons.com/ballpark-figure-meaning/

Pearson. (2022, May 5). *Everything but the Kitchen Sink – Meaning, Origin and Usage.* English-Grammar-Lessons.com. Retrieved September 15, 2022

Play hooky - Definition, Meaning & Synonyms. (n.d.). In *Vocabulary.com.* Retrieved September 15, 2022, from https://www.vocabulary.com/dictionary/play hooky

pop the question. (n.d.). Retrieved September 15, 2022, from https://www.theidioms.com/pop-the-question/

raise the bar. (n.d.). Retrieved September 15, 2022, from https://www.theidioms.com/raise-the-bar.

Rock the Boat | Phrase Definition, Origin & Examples. (n.d.). Retrieved September 15, 2022, from https://www.gingersoftware.com/content/phrases/rock-the-boat/

See eye to eye Idiom Definition. (2022, August 3). GRAMMARIST. Retrieved September 15, 2022, from https://grammarist.com/idiom/se e-eye-to-eye

Shrives, C. (n.d.). *"Back to Square One" | Origin and Meaning.* Retrieved September 15, 2022, from https://www.grammar-monster.com/sayin gs_proverbs/back_to_square_one.htm

Streat, S. (2016, March 21). *10 Business Idioms You Could Use In Your Next Presentation.* English With a Twist. Retrieved September 15, 2022, from https://englishwithatwist.com/2016/03/17/10-business-idioms-you-could-use-in-your-next-presentation/

Team, T. G. E. (2022, March 24). *English Idioms about Competition | Ginseng English | Learn English.* Ginseng English. Retrieved September 15, 2022, from https://ginsengenglish.com/blog/idioms-competition

TheIdioms.com. (n.d.). Retrieved September 15, 2022, from https://ww w.theidioms.com/

Touch base | ISO. (n.d.). Retrieved September 15, 2022, from https://iso. mit.edu/idioms/touch-base/

Training Industry, Inc. (2019, May 13). *Hitting the Nail on the Head: 7 English Idioms for Salespeople.* Training Industry. Retrieved September 15, 2022, from https://trainingindustry.com/articles/sales/hitting-the-nail-on-the-head-7-english-idioms-for-salespeople/

TUESDAY TRIVIA: Why Do We Cross Our Fingers for Good Luck? | PLANSPONSOR. (2021, November 16). Retrieved September 15, 2022

VOA Learning English. (2017, December 23). *"Don't Look a Gift Horse in the Mouth."* VOA. Retrieved September 15, 2022, from https://learningenglish.voanews.com/a/words-and-their-stories-dont-look-a-gift-horse-in-the-mouth

Wet blanket Idiom Definition. (2022, July 23). GRAMMARIST. Retrieved September 15, 2022, from https://grammarist.com/idiom/wet-blanket

Why are Bureaucratic Obstacles Referred to as "Red Tape"? (2016, May 4). Today I Found Out. Retrieved September 15, 2022, from https://www.todayifoundout.com/index.php/2016/05/bureaucratic-obstacles-referred-red-tape/

Word of mouth Idiom Definition. (2022, June 8). GRAMMARIST. Retrieved September 15, 2022, from https://grammarist.com/idiom/word-of-mouth.

you can't teach an old dog new tricks. (n.d.). Retrieved September 15, 2022, from https://www.theidioms.com/you-cant-teach-an-old-dog-new-tricks/

11

Chapter 11

12

Chapter 12